DOGS SET IX

SHETLAND SHEEPDOGS

Joanne Mattern
ABDO Publishing Company

Printed in the United States of America, North Mankato, Minnesota.
062011
092011

 PRINTED ON RECYCLED PAPER

Cover Photo: Mark Raycroft / Minden Pictures / National Geographic Stock
Interior Photos: Alamy pp. 5, 11, 13, 14, 16–17, 19; AP Images p. 7; Getty Images p. 12; Glow Images p. 21; iStockphoto p. 18; Thinkstock p. 9

Editors: Megan M. Gunderson, BreAnn Rumsch
Art Direction: Neil Klinepier

Library of Congress Cataloging-in-Publication Data

Mattern, Joanne, 1963-
  Shetland sheepdogs / Joanne Mattern.
      p. cm. -- (Dogs)
  Includes index.
  ISBN 978-1-61714-993-1
  1. Shetland sheepdog--Juvenile literature. I. Title.
  SF429.S62M27 2012
  636.737--dc22
                              2011009718

CONTENTS

THE DOG FAMILY

People all over the world keep dogs as pets. In fact, Americans alone own more than 75 million dogs! Worldwide, there are more than 400 different dog **breeds**.

Scientists believe all those breeds descended from the gray wolf. Both dogs and wolves are part of the family **Canidae**. This name comes from the Latin word *canis*, which means "dog."

For more than 12,000 years, dogs and people have lived and worked together. Over time, people **domesticated** dogs for hunting, herding, and guarding. Today, many dogs still do these and other important jobs.

A variety of dogs were bred to herd sheep. One of the most popular herding dogs is the Shetland sheepdog, or sheltie. This dog is a hard worker and a fun family pet.

Shetland sheepdogs may be wary of strangers, but they are very devoted to their families.

SHETLAND SHEEPDOGS

People have kept herds of sheep in Great Britain for hundreds of years. Dogs helped shepherds move herds from one place to another. The dogs also protected sheep from predators.

Shepherds used many dog **breeds** for this task, including the Border collie. Eventually, people brought the Border collie to Scotland's Shetland Islands. There, it bred with a small island dog called the Yakki. Later, it also bred with the King Charles spaniel and the Pomeranian.

In time, these mixed breed dogs developed into a new breed called the Shetland sheepdog. These tough little dogs herded sheep, helped on farms, and guarded homes.

The **American Kennel Club (AKC)** places shelties in its herding group. The AKC began registering the Shetland sheepdog in 1911. The first registered sheltie had been brought from Scotland to New York State. His name was Lord Scott.

Shelties are fast, graceful runners!

What They're Like

Shetland sheepdogs are highly intelligent. These playful dogs are easy to train and love to please their owners. They can even be taught to put away their own toys!

Because it is so smart, the Shetland sheepdog can get bored easily. This hardworking **breed** needs mental challenges. **Agility** competitions are a great choice. Keep a sheltie active and give it a job to do! This will help avoid problem behaviors such as excessive barking.

These loyal dogs want to be close to their owners. So, shelties are happiest when they get to be a part of family activities. They do not like to be left alone.

Shelties are always ready for fun. Yet these alert dogs can also be trained to be good watchdogs.

Shetland sheepdogs naturally love to chase things, including people! Unfortunately, they are also known to chase cars. So, shelties must be kept safe on a leash or in a fenced yard.

Shetland sheepdogs are one of the most popular breeds for agility competitions.

COAT AND COLOR

There are many possible colors for a Shetland sheepdog's coat. The **AKC** accepts black, **sable**, and blue **merle**. These colors are often marked with white or tan.

The Shetland sheepdog has a double coat that protects it from harsh weather. The outer coat is long, straight, and rough. It covers a soft, fluffy, thick inner coat.

The sheltie has a band of longer hair around the neck called a mane. There is thick hair on the rear end and the tail. The back of each leg is **feathered**. The hair on the feet, face, and tips of the ears is smooth.

All this hair can easily become tangled! So, a sheltie's coat needs weekly brushing to avoid becoming **matted**.

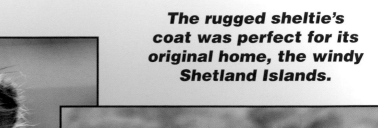

The rugged sheltie's coat was perfect for its original home, the windy Shetland Islands.

SIZE

Shetland sheepdogs are small, sturdy dogs. Males and females are similar in size. They usually weigh between 20 and 25 pounds (9 and 11 kg). For the **AKC**, they should stand 13 to 16 inches

(33 to 41 cm) tall at the shoulders.

The sheltie's wedge-shaped head tapers slightly to its black nose. The **muzzle** is rounded and the cheeks are flat. The tips of the sheltie's pointed ears flop forward. This dog's medium-sized, almond-shaped eyes are usually dark. But, blue **merle** shelties can have blue or merle eyes.

The small Shetland sheepdog was bred to guard the small sheep of the Shetland Islands.

The Shetland sheepdog's muscular neck holds its head high. Its strong legs support a level back and a deep chest. The long, fluffy tail hangs down along the back legs. But if a sheltie is alert, it holds its tail high!

CARE

Shelties like to be active! They need daily exercise. It is a good idea to let them play outside in a fenced area, if possible. In fact, these talented jumpers often do well at **agility** training.

With all that activity, caring for a sheltie's coat is very important. Along with weekly brushing, baths are necessary if the dog gets very dirty. Be sure to use a shampoo made just for dogs. A slight trim can help keep the coat tidy. Brushing a sheltie's teeth regularly will also help keep the dog healthy.

Regular health checks are another way to prevent illness in your Shetland sheepdog. The veterinarian will give your dog **vaccines**. He or she will **spay** or **neuter** a sheltie around six months of age if the dog is not going to be **bred**.

Shelties are generally healthy, but they can have a few serious medical issues. Some dogs experience vision or hearing problems. They can also suffer from **hip dysplasia**.

Grooming your puppy will make it more comfortable with grooming as an adult.

FEEDING

Whatever its **breed**, each dog has its own dietary needs. They depend on the dog's age, size, and activity level. Overfeeding is harmful. So, be sure your sheltie gets the right amount of food to maintain a healthy weight.

Shetland sheepdogs need high-quality food to stay healthy and strong. They can eat dry, wet, or

semimoist varieties. A puppy might eat three small meals a day. An adult dog can have one or two larger meals.

Shelties also need plenty of water to stay healthy. Dog owners should always have a bowl of clean, fresh water available for their pets to drink. Just like you, dogs especially need a drink during hot weather or after exercising.

A veterinarian or a breeder can suggest the best diet for your dog.

THINGS THEY NEED

Be sure your dog's toys are not too small, so they can't be swallowed.

Shetland sheepdogs were **bred** to be workers. Their strong bodies need exercise every day! Make time to walk and play with your pet. A sheltie should also have toys to play with, especially while you are away.

Hard rubber balls or hollow chew toys stuffed with treats provide hours of entertainment.

Obedience training is important for all dogs. Shetland sheepdogs are devoted to their owners and will want to obey them. Training develops well-behaved pets and prevents destructive habits such as chewing furniture. It is also important for shelties to be **socialized**.

All dogs need a leash, a collar, and license and identification tags. They need food and water bowls, too. Owners should also provide a crate. A crate pad or a bed gives the sheltie a comfortable place to sleep.

A crate gives a sheltie a safe place to stay.

PUPPIES

Shetland sheepdog mothers are **pregnant** for about 63 days. On average, there are seven puppies in a **litter**.

Sheltie puppies cannot see or hear until they are two to three weeks old. Their mother cares for them at first, but they should soon have human contact too. The puppies are big enough to go to a new home when they are six to eight weeks old.

You can get a sheltie from a **breeder**, a rescue group, or an animal shelter. A healthy puppy should be active, alert, bright-eyed, and curious. It should have clean, soft skin under its fluffy fur. The puppy should not be too **aggressive** or too shy.

When you get your puppy home, it is important to **socialize** it. Introduce the puppy to people and to other animals. Take the puppy to different places such as the park or the pet store. With the right care and training, a Shetland sheepdog will be a loving family member for about 14 years.

Socializing your puppy will make it comfortable outside its home.

GLOSSARY

aggressive (uh-GREH-sihv) - displaying hostility.

agility - a sport in which a handler leads a dog through an obstacle course during a timed race.

American Kennel Club (AKC) - an organization that studies and promotes interest in purebred dogs.

breed - a group of animals sharing the same ancestors and appearance. A breeder is a person who raises animals. Raising animals is often called breeding them.

Canidae (KAN-uh-dee) - the scientific Latin name for the dog family. Members of this family are called canids. They include wolves, jackals, foxes, coyotes, and domestic dogs.

domesticated - adapted to life with humans.

feathered - having a fringe of hair.

hip dysplasia (HIHP dihs-PLAY-zhuh) - unusual formation of the hip joint.

litter - all of the puppies born at one time to a mother dog.

matted - forming a tangled mass.

merle - having dark patches of color on a lighter background.

22

muzzle - an animal's nose and jaws.

neuter (NOO-tuhr) - to remove a male animal's reproductive glands.

pregnant - having one or more babies growing within the body.

sable - having black-tipped hairs on a silver, gold, gray, fawn, or brown background.

socialize - to accustom an animal or a person to spending time with others.

spay - to remove a female animal's reproductive organs.

vaccine (vak-SEEN) - a shot given to prevent illness or disease.

WEB SITES

To learn more about Shetland sheepdogs, visit ABDO Publishing Company online. Web sites about Shetland sheepdogs are featured on our Book Links page. These links are routinely monitored and updated to provide the most current information available.

www.abdopublishing.com

INDEX